Contents

KT-376-403

The dinosaurs

Dinosaurs were reptiles.

Dinosaurs

Triceratops

Daniel Nunn

C032639678

www.heinemann.co.uk/library

Visit our website to find out more information about Heinemann Lib

To order:

☎ Phone 44 (0) 1865 888066

  Send a fax to 44 (0) 1865 314091

📄 Visit the Heinemann Bookshop at www.heinemann.co.uk/library to

💻 catalogue and order online.

HAMPSHIRE COUNTY LIBRARY	
C032 639 678	
Peters	28-Apr-2008
J567	£5.25
9780431184548	

First published in Great Britain by Heinemann Library,
Halley Court, Jordan Hill, Oxford OX2 8EJ, part of Harcourt
Education. Heinemann is a registered trademark of Harcourt
Education Ltd.

© Harcourt Education Ltd 2007
First published in paperback in 2008
The moral right of the proprietor has been asserted.

All rights reserved. No part of this publication may be
reproduced, stored in a retrieval system, or transmitted in any
form or by any means, electronic, mechanical, photocopying,
recording, or otherwise, without either the prior written
permission of the publishers or a licence permitting restricted
copying in the United Kingdom issued by the Copyright
Licensing Agency Ltd, 90 Tottenham Court Road, London
W1T 4LP (www.cla.co.uk).

Editorial: Daniel Nunn and Rachel Howells
Illustrations: James Field of Simon Girling and Associates
Design: Joanna Hinton-Malivoire
Picture research: Erica Newbery
Production: Duncan Gilbert

Printed and bound in China by South China
Printing Co. Ltd.

10 digit ISBN 0 431 18447 X (hardback)
13 digit ISBN 978 0431 184470 (hardback)

11 10 09 08 07
10 9 8 7 6 5 4 3 2 1

10 digit ISBN 0 431 18454 2 (paperback)
13 digit ISBN 978 0431 184548 (paperback)

12 11 10 09 08
10 9 8 7 6 5 4 3 2 1

British Library Cataloguing in Publication Data
Nunn, Daniel
Triceratops. – (Dinosaurs)
567.9'158
A full catalogue record for this book is available from the
British Library.

Acknowledgements
The publishers would like to thank the following for
permission to reproduce photographs: Alamy pp. 6, and 23
(Christian Darkin), 14 (Jeff Morgan), 19 (Phototake Inc.),
20 (JupiterMedia); Corbis pp. 7 (Gary W. Carter), 18 and
23 (Annie Griffiths Belt), 21 (Paul A. Souders), 22 (Louie
Psihoyos), 22 (Philip Gould); Science Photo Library p. 12
(Christian Darkin).

Cover photograph of Triceratops reproduced with
permission of Alamy/Christian Darkin.

Every effort has been made to contact copyright holders
of any material reproduced in this book. Any omissions will
be rectified in subsequent printings if notice is given to the
publishers.

Dinosaurs lived long ago.

Triceratops was a dinosaur.
Triceratops lived long ago.

Today there are no Triceratops.

Triceratops

Protoceratops

Some dinosaurs were small.

But Triceratops was big.

Triceratops had thick, strong legs.

Triceratops lived together in herds.

Triceratops walked slowly most
of the time.

But Triceratops could run
fast, too.

horn

Triceratops had three horns.

Triceratops used its horns to fight other dinosaurs.

But Triceratops did not eat
other dinosaurs.

Triceratops ate bushes and plants.

How do we know?

Scientists have found fossils
of Triceratops.

Fossils are the bones of animals which have turned to rock.

fossil

Fossils show us the outline
of the dinosaur.

Triceratops

Fossils tell us what Triceratops was like.

Fossil quiz

A

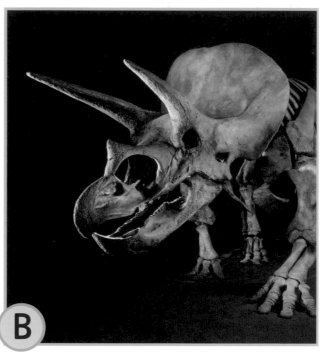

B

One of these fossils was Triceratops. Can you tell which one? Turn to page 24 to find out the answer.

Picture glossary

 **dinosaur** a reptile who lived millions of years ago

 **fossil** part of a dead plant or animal that has become hard like rock

 **horn** a hard pointed growth on the heads of some animals

 **reptile** a cold-blooded animal

Index

Answer to question on page 22
Fossil B was Triceratops.
Fossil A was Tyrannosaurus rex.

Note to Parents and Teachers
Before reading
Talk to the children about dinosaurs. Do they know the names of any dinosaurs? What
features did they have e.g. long neck, bony plates, sharp teeth? Has anyone seen a dinosaur
fossil or model in a museum?

After reading
- Measuring in the playground
  Tell the children that some dinosaurs were larger than the classroom. Give them a ball
  of wool to measure Triceratops (11 metres), Diplodocus (28 metres), Brachiosaurus
  (25 metres). Staple the lengths of wool to the classroom walls.
- Make a head band for each child. Ask them to draw the head of a dinosaur onto card
  and cut it out. Tell them to decorate the headband and then staple the dinosaur head
  onto the band.
- Read a fiction book to the children e.g. *Harry and the Bucket Full of Dinosaurs* by
  Ian Whybrow (Puffin).